# INGLIS ALLEN

# OFFICIAL CELTIC ANNUAL 1999

**Written by**
Douglas G. Russell

Edited by John C. Traynor

Printed and Published by Inglis Allen Ltd.
© 1998 Inglis Allen Ltd. All Rights Reserved.

ISBN 1-89959-905-3

£5.99

CONTENTS

# THE DYNAMO

## CRAIG BURLEY

**I**n truth, the announcement came as no great surprise. The Scottish Football Writers' Association had confirmed Celtic's dynamo, Craig Burley, as 'Player Of The Year'. Only twelve months earlier, the player had been omitted from the Chelsea team and FA Cup glory at Wembley. What a difference a year makes!

The midfield maestro had shone like a beacon throughout the 1998 campaign, revealing a resolve second to none. A winner in the true sense of the word.

Craig's ten league goals included the winners against Hearts, Dundee United and Aberdeen in December, January and March respectively. He was also the only Celtic player to notch four 'doubles'

in that historic season. The first came against SC Tirol in the UEFA Cup (6-3, August 1997), followed by three in the premiership against Motherwell (3-2, September 1997 and 4-1, April 1998) and Hibernian (5-0, December 1997). Of course, it would be criminal not to mention the small matter of his opening goal against a certain team in blue at Celtic Park early in January!

Probably one game sums up Craig Burley more than any other – the aforementioned 4-1 defeat of Motherwell in April 1998, nearing the season's end. Celtic's visitors that day had taken an early lead before the 'dynamo' turned on the power to score twice before the interval. In the second half, he then 'made' the other two. Truly a performance and a half.

Many are convinced that, in time, Craig Burley will become one of the Celtic 'greats'. Of course, only the passing of years can verify something like that.

One thing is certain, though. If such accolades were based on the events of just one season, he would already be one.

# THE DYNAMO

Craig Burley's late winner against Hearts at Celtic Park, 13.12.97.

# DONNELLY DOES IT!

## SIMON DONNELLY

The war of nerves between Celtic and Rangers in the race for the Premiership trophy was at a crucial stage. Sandwiched between Scottish Cup and League matches with their greatest rivals, the 'Bhoys' faced a perilous evening trip to Kilmarnock in early April. At this point, both contenders had accumulated sixty-three points, with the Ibrox club having played one more game.

The Celts were desperate to secure the obvious benefit of a three-point cushion before the following Sunday's tough visit to Govan.

Rugby Park is never an easy venue and so it was proving to be when, early in the second half, Killie's Burke scored to cancel out Henrik Larsson's opener. Step forward Simon Donnelly with a delightful goal. Following a lovely passing movement involving five Celts, young Simon finished it off with a delectable chip and victory was assured.

The striker had notched several crucial goals that season, including the extra-time away winner against St. Johnstone in the 'Coca-Cola' Cup third round match. A total of sixteen goals in all competitions (three Scottish and one European) ensured Simon's position just behind Henrik Larsson in that particular chart.

The player capped a fine season with his beloved club by becoming the youngest member of Craig Brown's Scotland Squad in France for the World Cup.

Nobody could question his right to be there.

# 1Ø-IN-A-ROW

**Premier League, 9th May 1998**

**CELTIC 2**                    **ST. JOHNSTONE 0**
Larsson (3 mins)
Brattbakk (72 mins)

**A**nd so, finally, on 9th May 1998 in the East End of Glasgow, Celtic were crowned the new Premier League Champions in front of their legions of fans. Insert 'loyal' before 'fans' and underline! The best team in Scotland had eventually triumphed in a fairytale ending.

Before the last game of the season, Celtic, on 74 points, were 2 ahead of their oldest rivals and reigning champions, Rangers. The 'Bhoys' knew that a home victory over St. Johnstone would be enough, regardless of results elsewhere. Defeat the team from Perth and everything else was irrelevant.

Few of the assembled masses could have anticipated such a dramatic opening to the game in only three minutes. Taking a Lambert pass, Henrik Larsson cut inside and, almost nonchalantly, unleashed a

*Harald Brattbakk seals the Championship.*

*Henrik Larsson's stunning opener.*

tremendous twenty-yard drive that flew past Alan Main in the St. Johnstone goal. The jubilant crowd could hardly believe their eyes. Their heroes were already one up.

The anticipated avalanche failed to materialise, however, and although Henrik was unfortunate not to score again after chipping the goalkeeper, the scoreline remained the same after forty-five minutes.

Such was the fans' anxiety that time seemed to stand still during those long minutes of the second period. Everything would soon change, nevertheless, with a goal of real quality. Tom Boyd fed Jackie McNamara perfectly down the right. His subsequent low cross was calmly finished by substitute Harald Brattbakk. Simple, yet brilliant, and it was all over. The final fifteen minutes passed quickly in song and celebration.

Maybe it was not a vintage Celtic performance but that hardly mattered as the Championship was returning to Celtic Park. Seven of the fourteen players involved that day were in their first season with the club and that surely augurs well for the future.

Those with Celtic in their hearts had waited a long, long time for this day and they would not be denied their say, or even shedding a few tears as the emotion of the moment sunk in.

In the words of the No. 1 song – 'Such A Perfect Day'.

Celtic had scaled this particular mountain. Greater challenges now lay ahead.

CHAMPIONS

CHAMPIONS
CELTIC F.C.
1Ø
IN A ROW

CHAMPIONS

CHAMPIONS

# CHAMPIONS

# THE PLAYERS' CHOICE

## JACKIE McNAMARA

It was surely one of the proudest moments of his career when Jackie McNamara was named 'Player Of The Year' for Season 1997/98 by his fellow professionals. He had become the seventh Celt to win this award behind Davie Provan (1980), Charlie Nicholas (1983), Brian McClair (1987), Paul McStay (1988), Paul Elliot (1991) and Paolo di Canio (1997).

This wasn't the youthful Celt's first taste of such honour as, two years previously, at the ripe old age of twenty-two, he had captured the 'Young Player' trophy. Quite a double! Jackie had, indeed, come a long way since that career-threatening injury back in March 1989 when, during a training session, his right leg was shattered in two places.

Like all the Celts, Jackie ended the long league campaign on a high with a medal but all his performances that year had been champion. Who can forget his goal against Liverpool in the UEFA Cup first round tie at Celtic Park, when the English outfit were most fortunate to escape with a draw despite scoring first that night? Pity he was forced to miss the return leg at Anfield two weeks later.

The player notched two other goals in the season – in the 5-0 rout of Hibernian pre-Christmas and the 1-1 draw with Hearts at Tynecastle in early February. Both strikes were recorded during a quite dazzling run of form when, over a period of some months, week in and week out, McNamara performed at a consistently high standard. His place in the Scotland Squad for the World Cup Finals in France during the summer was due reward. The 'Champions' League' also beckoned of course.

Another year on a par with the 97/98 Season and the fans will be more than delighted. Well, the home fans, anyway!

*Above: Jackie scoring in the 5-0 victory over Hibs in late December, 1997.*

**F U N Z**

**Q U I Z**

1. Marc Rieper and Craig Burley signed from which London clubs?

2. Celtic conceded fewer goals than any other team in the Premier League. How few?

3. Paul Lambert won a European Cup medal with which club?

4. Who was top scorer against Rangers in all competitions?

5. Stephane Mahe scored only once in the season. Against which club?

6. How many games did Jonathan Gould miss after appearing for the first time in the opening home league game of the season?

7. Who scored Celtic's winner in the 3-2 Scottish Cup victory at Tannadice?

8. Marc Rieper scored for Denmark in the World Cup Finals against which team?

9. Henrik Larsson was top scorer in all competitions. How many goals did he record?

10. Who won the 'Head of the Year' prize from the Scottish Hairdressers' Federation?

Answers on Page 62

*Super Celt*
*Darren Jackson*

*Super Celt*
*Morten Wieghorst*

# SEARCH FOR A HERO

## HENRIK LARSSON

**A**ny footballing debut is fraught with danger. Like walking through a minefield, every step is potentially hazardous. Just ask Henrik Larsson.

The Swede's first appearance in the green was against Hibernian at Easter Road in the first league game of the season, substituting Andy Thom. It is well documented that his misplaced pass found Chic Charnley, who then netted for his team's winner. Given a choice in retrospect, the ex-Feyenoord star woud surely have stayed on the bench!

There was little improvement the following week, when Henrik started the game – Dunfermline won 2-1 at Celtic Park. The pressure was now on – but this was nothing new to Larsson. Earlier in his career, playing for his country, the Swede was involved in the quarter-final penalty 'shoot-out' with Romania in the 1994 World Cup. Now <u>that's</u> pressure! Henrik converted his spot-kick and Sweden were in the semi-final.

After those first two league setbacks, the player struck a rich vein of form and his contribution to the team was of prime importance. In fact, he became an 'ever-present' in the starting line-up until 27th December in Perth – the day St. Johnstone beat Celtic 1-0. Henrik returned the following week for Celtic's crucial 'Ne'erday' encounter with Rangers and never missed a game after that.

The Swede struck three 'doubles' in the season against Aberdeen (2-0, September 1997), Kilmarnock (4-0, October 1997) and Dundee United (4-0, November 1997). A total of 19 goals in all tournaments were accredited to him on his way to becoming the 'Bhoys' top scorer.

Most fans, of course, would rather recall just one particular goal from the campaign. No prizes for guessing which one.

*Henrik Larsson scores against Kilmarnock and (below) Hibs.*

# SEARCH FOR A HERO

# CELTS

# CELEBRATE

# JUDGEMENT DAY

**Premier League, 2nd January 1998**

**CELTIC 2**              **RANGERS 0**

Burley (66 mins)
Lambert (87 mins)

**T**here could be no half measures. Quite simply, Celtic just had to win this crucial 'Ne'erday' fixture in order to stay in the Championship race.

Prior to this day's game, arch rivals Rangers were already four points clear at the top of the Premier League. A victory for the team from Govan would obviously put them seven points ahead and thus create a gap too great to contemplate with less than half of the fixture programme remaining. The pressure was all on Celtic.

The 'Hoops' grew in stature as the game progressed and, after half an hour, began to dominate and take control. It was a relieved Rangers side that reached the safety of the interval still level. The second half would prove, however, that there was no hiding place!

*Craig Burley opens the scoring.*

*Paul Lambert's stunning goal.*

Just after the break, following Jackie McNamara's neat reverse pass, Craig Burley opened the scoring with his first-ever 'Old Firm' goal. Celtic Park erupted with a sound like a stormcloud thunderclap. It was almost beyond belief.

After that, it was all one-way traffic with Paul Lambert, Craig Burley and Morten Wieghorst in total midfield control. By this time, Enrico Annoni had already snuffed out the danger of Laudrup and striker Negri was, as they say, 'in the back pocket' of Marc Rieper. (In fact, in the Dane's sixteen appearances for Celtic, only eight goals had been conceded).

Such was the total superiority of the home side, it was now just a question of how many goals the 'Bhoys' could score. Although Harald Brattbakk had chances to increase the tally, it was Paul Lambert who sent the crowd into a state of delirium. With only three minutes remaining, his astonishing, swerving strike from far out left 'keeper Goram clawing at air as the ball buried itself in the corner of a bulging net. Victory was complete and comprehensive.

Rangers' lead at the top of the division was now just one solitary point. Celtic had passed the test, winning this traditional fixture for the first time in the ten years since January 1988. Ironically, this was the season when the 'Hoops' had last won the Championship. Maybe the tide had turned at last.

Suffice to say that there would be twists galore between then and the end of the campaign at Celtic Park in early May. On this January day, however, the legions in green and white celebrated a famous triumph. That was more than enough . . . . . . for now.

# THE QUIET MAN

## MARC RIEPER

**T**he signing of Dane, Marc Rieper, from West Ham in September 1997, proved to be inspirational. With Alan Stubbs already entrenched in the Celtic rearguard, the 'Old Bhoy' and the new arrival combined well to form, in due course, the best central defensive partnership in Scotland.

Marc was hugely impressive right from the start and, following his first sixteen games to the end of the year, only a meagre eight goals had been conceded. Next in line would be champions Rangers at Celtic Park on 2nd January, a game of crucial importance to the 'Hoops'.

Prior to this match, Rangers' Italian import, Marco Negri, had scored an amazing thirty Premier League goals (including three in the previous two games) and was, obviously, in a rich vein of form. Suffice to say that, at the end of the ninety minutes, the striker's total had not increased as Marc had policed him right out of the game.

The defender seemed to grow in stature as the season progressed and even scored the winner in the 1-0 victory at Easter Road in late February. Of course, his previous goal for the 'Hoops' was the all-important opener in the 'Coca-Cola' Cup Final victory over Dundee United in November.

In early May, for obvious reasons, Marc became the 'Grin Rieper', as that elusive league title was finally secured.

However, he barely had time to reflect on his first successful season in Scotland before heading off to France (accompanied by fellow-Celt and fellow-Dane, Morten Wieghorst) as an integral member of his country's World Cup Squad. Indeed, in Denmark's opening tie, the defender headed home the winner against opponents, Saudi Arabia. The 'Quiet Man' had captured the headlines.

Even though he goes about his business with the minimum of fuss, Marc Rieper is a major talent. That's for sure.

Super Celt
Enrico Annoni

Super Celt
Stephane Mahe

# FIVE-IN-A-ROW

## HARALD BRATTBAKK

It may not be up to the high standard of 'University Challenge' but how about quizzing your friends with this 'starter for ten' – name the only Celtic first team player who has won five consecutive championship medals and, therefore, can claim his own unique 'Five-In-A-Row'?

Step forward 'Hitman', Harald Brattbakk, who had previously enjoyed four League Championship triumphs with Rosenborg in Norway prior to signing for the 'Hoops' in December last year. Some five months later, on a glorious day in Glasgow, it was number five.

However, it had not all been plain sailing since crossing the water

*Harald scoring against Dunfermline both 'away' and (above opposite) at 'home'.*

to Scotland. Football can be a cruel master, as certain players tend to be criticised regardless of their contribution. Such was the case with Brattbakk on occasion – but the elegant striker has come a long way in silencing his critics.

Celtic played both Kilmarnock and Dunfermline at home, in late February, in the space of four days. Harald Brattbakk was exceptional in both games, claiming all four goals in the 4-0 demolition of the Ayrshire club and scoring twice in the 5-1 thrashing handed out to the Fifers. Only a select few top-class strikers ever net six goals in two games!

Fast forward to the last game of the season, when history was in the making. The striker was surely the coolest man on the park as he swept the ball past Alan Main to relieve the Parkhead tension. The image of the player, arms aloft in 'Victory V' celebration, will remain etched in the mind for a long time.

**Harald Brattbakk had finally arrived.**

# CHAMPIONSHIP

*Simon Donnelly v. Motherwell, 18.4.98.*

*Henrik Larsson v. Aberdeen, 2.2.98*

# GOALS

*Craig Burley v. Motherwell, 18.4.98.*

*Regi Blinker v. Dunfermline, 1.11.97.*

# CHAMPIONSHIP GOALS QUIZ

1. Who scored Celtic's first and last goals of the league season?

2. The 'Hoops' scored five goals in each of two games. Can you name their opponents?

3. Henrik Larsson was the club's top scorer in the league. With how many goals?

4. Celtic beat Kilmarnock 4-0 in February. What was so special that day?

5. Who scored for Celtic in the 'Coca-Cola' Cup Final?

6. Swede, Henrik Larsson, notched three 'doubles' in the months of September, October and November. Against which teams?

7. Paul Lambert scored with stunning strikes in two consecutive games. Can you name Celtic's opponents?

8. Name, the two foreign players who scored 'doubles' against Dundee United in November?

9. Apart from Henrik Larsson, identify the two other players who reached double figures in the league scoring charts.

10. Goal of the season?

Answers on Page 62

# GOAL OF

*Celtic Park, 9th May 1998. Celtic's first goal against St. Johnstone.*

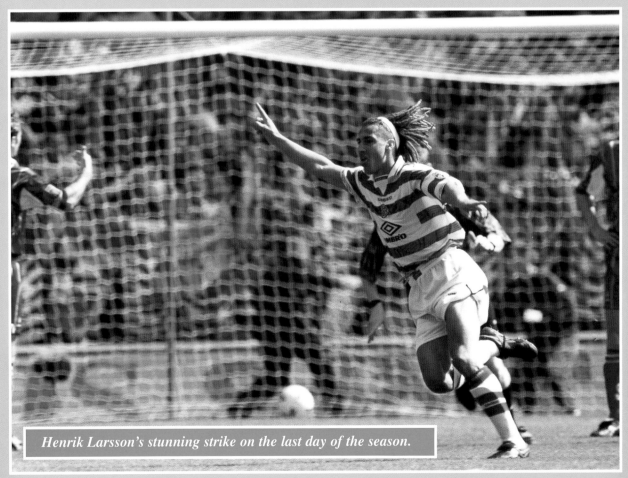

*Henrik Larsson's stunning strike on the last day of the season.*

# SILVER LINING

Coca-Cola Cup Final, 30th November 1997

**CELTIC 3**   **DUNDEE UNITED 0**

Rieper (21 mins)
Larsson (23 mins)
Burley (59 mins)

Celtic's 'Never-Say-Die' attitude is known to all, for, as a football team, they are never beaten until the sound of the final whistle. This day, however, it was not necessary to call upon that special quality to secure the first silverware of the season, the 'Coca-Cola' Cup. Quite simply, the game was effectively over after some twenty-three minutes – in a two-minute spell that ended a fifteen-year wait!

Opponents on the day, Dundee United, began well enough but were soon in trouble, courtesy of that well known Danish double-act

*Craig Burley scores goal No. 3.*

'Wieghorst and Rieper'. Marc's headed goal from Morten's excellent cross lit up the Ibrox scoreboard. The lead had hardly been registered before the 'Hoops' struck again with Henrik Larsson's strike from outside the penalty area. Two goals in two minutes and the game was dead.

To be fair, the Tayside men appeared more determined in the second half but it was to no avail. Celtic were still the team more likely to score and so it transpired with half an hour remaining. Craig Burley, with a bullet header, made it three. At this point, the Dundee United players just wanted it all to end and be on their way home.

For Celtic, it had proved to be a fine <u>team</u> performance, with all three goalscorers new signings that season. 'Man of the Match' Morten Wieghorst was immense and seemed to grow stronger as the game progressed – but, in truth, there wasn't a weakness in green.

This victory would be accorded its rightful place in the record books, as it was the club's first League Cup Final triumph since 1982. But, of course, the 'Holy Grail' for this season was the Championship.

Celtic knew that it was by their title challenge that, ultimately, they would be judged.

# SILVER LINING

# THE GLASGOW CUP

**T**his spectacular trophy, which once ranked, together with the Glasgow Charity Cup (present whereabouts unknown), amongst Scotland's premier senior football competitions, was won by Celtic twenty-nine times in its heyday. In those days, Glasgow Cup matches, featuring such now-sadly-defunct outfits as Third Lanark as well as Celtic, Rangers and the other senior Glasgow clubs, attracted crowds to rival any event in the football calendar. It was a tournament of genuine prestige, as its imposing appearance proudly proclaims.

Sadly, with the passage of time, the Glasgow Cup drifted into something of a non-event, as the advent of European football, with the glamorous occasions generated, drew the focus away from minor domestic competition. A once-proud contest had become something of a joke, paid scant attention by clubs and public alike.

Only in recent years has the historic old 'pot' had some of its former pride, if not prestige, restored. It is now contested by the young lions of the Glasgow clubs' under-18 sides and keenly contested at that, attracting large, enthusiastic crowds looking for an early glimpse of the stars of the future.

Height: 31 1/2"

# MIDFIELD MAESTRO

## PAUL LAMBERT

In theory, a footballer's career is one of constant development and learning but, of course, in practice this is not always the case. As a rule, very few Scottish players ever have the opportunity to perform at the top level in Germany and thus develop their skills.

Paul Lambert proved the exception to that particular rule when the midfielder joined crack outfit, Borussia Dortmund, after leaving Motherwell. By the end of Season 1996/97, Paul was the proud owner of a European Cup Winner's medal following his club's triumph in the final of the competition, when Juventus were beaten. This was richly deserved as the player had performed consistently well throughout the

'Champions League' series of games leading up to the match against the Italian giants.

There is little doubt that, when Paul Lambert returned to his native land and signed for Celtic in November '97, he was a far more assured player. Certainly, fans of the 'Hoops' took to him immediately. Although they had to wait until early January for his first goal, it was, to say the least, worth the wait!

In the traditional 'Ne'erday' encounter with Rangers, Celtic were cruising to victory as the game reached its climax, even tho' the 'Bhoys' were only one goal in front. Paul chose his moment with only three minutes to go and let fly with a thunderous, dipping strike, leaving Goram (so often Rangers' saviour in the past) helpless. A wonder goal.

Obviously not content with that, the Celtic star repeated this particular dose of medicine the following week against his old club, Motherwell, in the 1-1 draw at Fir Park. The only difference was that, on this occasion, many fans considered it an even better strike!

Paul ended the Scottish season with another five-star display in the Championship clincher against St. Johnstone. In the summer of 1998, he was one of several Celtic players with the Scotland Squad in France for the World Cup. It came as no great surprise that in the first game, with reigning champions, Brazil, he was in the eyes of many, 'Man Of The Match'.

No mean feat at that level!

# PAUL
# LAMBERT

# A CAPTAIN'S PART

## TOM BOYD

**S**ometimes the years pass slowly. On the other hand, time can often fly by. No doubt in the six-year period since Tom Boyd arrived at Celtic Park from Chelsea, it had been more of the former due to the dominance in Scotland of a certain club.

But that chain had now been well and truly broken and, as he proudly held aloft the Championship trophy on Saturday 9th May, the Celtic captain surely wished that particular moment would last forever.

Of course, that was not the only silverware Tom received on Celtic's behalf during the season, as the 'Coca-Cola' Cup already sat comfortably in the club's trophy room. "Two out of three ain't bad," as the song says.

The 'Boyd Bhoy' had been a stalwart all year, with barely a single poor game. Like several others, Tom had excelled in the 'Old Firm' clash of 2nd January. Celtic's victory that day proved to be a major turning point in the quest for glory.

A true captain playing a captain's part.

*Tom Boyd, captain of Celtic.*

# THE SILVER

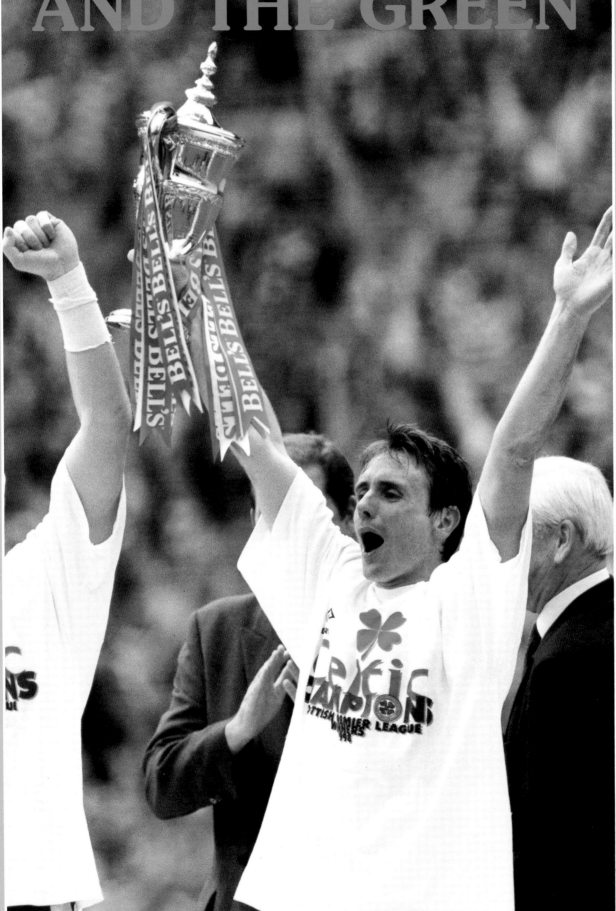

# SAFETY FIRST

## JONATHAN GOULD

**A**lthough it is a long way from Bradford to Paris, most people could complete the journey to the French capital in a matter of hours. It took the Celtic 'keeper, Jonathan Gould, almost a year . . . . . . and he was still absolutely delighted!

Back in the summer of 1997, a bronzed Gould was on holiday in Magaluf, celebrating the fact that Bradford (his team) had avoided relegation from the English First Division. Some twelve months later, following a call-up to the Scotland World Cup Squad for France as a replacement for Andy Goram, it was indeed a whole new world.

Celtic had given Jonathan's career a new boost. When the call came to join the club, he was Bradford's third-choice 'keeper. One year on and the player had been shortlisted by the Scottish Football Writers' Association for their 'Player Of The Year' award.

Jonathan first appeared in the 'No. 1' jersey for the 'Bhoys' back in August, against Berwick Rangers in the 'Coca-Cola' Cup second round tie. From then until that famous last game of the season against St. Johnstone, he never missed a game, conceding only twenty-two League Championship goals. During that time, the 'keeper had developed a fine understanding with both central defenders, Alan Stubbs and Marc Rieper. The case for the defence was complete.

The secret of Celtic's success in the 1998 Championship was built around a supreme <u>team</u> effort. An integral part of that had been the quietly confident displays of Mr Jonathan Gould.

*Jonathan Gould in action against Kilmarnock and (Above) Dunfermline*

# ANSWERS

## FUN QUIZ

**1.** West Ham and Chelsea.   **2.** Only 24 goals in 36 games.   **3.** Borussia Dortmund.
**4.** Craig Burley scored in both the 2-0 'Ne'erday' victory and the 2-1 Scottish Cup defeat.
**5.** Dunfermline (2-1, Scottish Cup, 16.2.98).   **6.** None.   **7.** Erik Pedersen – it was an
'own goal'.   **8.** Saudi Arabia.   **9.** 19 goals (16 in the League and 3 in the 'Coca-Cola'
Cup).   **10.** Simon Donnelly.

## CHAMPIONSHIP GOALS QUIZ

**1.** Malky Mackay and Harald Brattbakk.   **2.** Hibernian (5-0, 20.12.97) and
Dunfermline (5-1, 25.2.98).   **3.** 16 goals.   **4.** Harald Brattbakk scored all four
goals.   **5.** Marc Rieper, Henrik Larsson and Craig Burley.   **6.** Aberdeen (2-0,
20.9.97), Kilmarnock (4-0, 4.10.97) and Dundee United (4-0, 22.11.97).
**7.** Rangers (2-0, 2.1.98) and Motherwell (1-1, 10.2.98).   **8.** Henrik Larsson and
Andy Thom.   **9.** Craig Burley and Simon Donnelly, with 10 each.   **10.** Take your
pick – they were all important.

## PHOTO FUN QUIZ

**1.**      Page 21 – Jackie McNamara, Harald Brattbakk and Craig Burley.
**2.** Page 41 – Gerry Creaney and Charlie Nicholas.

## ACKNOWLEDGEMENTS

Designed by Douglas Russell, with special assistance from Lisa Russell.

Typesetting and Origination by Inglis Allen, Kirkcaldy.

Bound in Scotland by Hunter & Foulis, Edinburgh.

All photographs supplied by The Sun (Picture Editor: Mark Sweeney).

Every effort has been made by the publishers to ensure the accuracy of all details and
information in this publication.

Printed and Published in Scotland by

# INGLIS ALLEN

40 Townsend Place, Kirkcaldy, Fife, Scotland KY1 1HF.
Telephone (01592) 267201    Fax (01592) 206049    ISDN (01592) 646166
ISBN 1-89959-905-3 © Inglis Allen 1998. All rights reserved.